ANIMAL PREDATORS

Mountain Lions

SANDRA MARKLE

LERNER PUBLICATIONS COMPANY / MINNEAPOLIS

The Animal World is Full of
PREDATORS.

Predators are the hunters that find, catch, and eat other animals—their prey—in order to survive. Every environment has its chain of hunters. The smaller, slower, less able predators become prey for the bigger, faster, more cunning hunters. And everywhere, there are just a few kinds of predators at the top of the food chain. In western North America, Central America, and South America, one of these top predators is the mountain lion. *Mountain lions are also called by many other names, including cougar, puma, catamount, panther, painter, ghost cat, king cat, yellow tiger, and screamer.*

It's late June in Montana, but snow still lingers in the high forests. In open patches, new green sprouts peek through the winter brown grass. The tawny brown female mountain lion blends in perfectly. She moves slowly— almost silently—on big, padded paws, stalking a mule deer that's grazing just ahead of her.

All the while, the mountain lion's keen senses keep her focused on her prey and alert to any threats, such as wolves or a grizzly bear. Her sharp senses are one of the reasons she's such a good hunter. Her big eyes give her a wide-angle view, and she can see details clearly even in dim light. Her ears, high on top of her head, can each turn separately. They can pick up the slightest noise, including the high-pitched squeak of a mouse. Even her sense of smell, which isn't as keen as a wolf's or a bear's, is still sharp. So she stays aware of everything happening around her as she sneaks up on her prey.

When she's close enough, she starts to run. Like releasing a stretched rubber band, the big cat's powerful hind leg muscles launch her forward.

Her prey, the female mule deer, starts running too. Deer are built to run fast and twist and turn quickly to escape. But for short distances, a mountain lion can sprint faster—as fast as 35 miles (56 kilometers) per hour. The mountain lion has a very flexible spine. This lets her swerve easily and closely follow her prey. Her long tail helps her stay balanced. Hunter and prey run flat out. Each is running for its life.

Then the big cat leaps. Her leap carries her more than 20 feet (12 meters) to her prey's side. While she was running, the big cat's claws were retracted, or pulled into her paws, to protect them. As she grabs the deer's shoulder and neck, she pushes her toe tips downward, digging in her needle-sharp claws.

The deer bleats, and its front legs buckle. The mountain lion bites, driving her long canine teeth into the deer's spine. She severs the deer's spine to make the kill. Then she drags her prey to a more sheltered spot. This is not an easy task. The deer weighs as much or more than she does. But hidden, the mountain lion can eat with less chance of being spotted by other predators. A wolf pack or a bear could attack and drive her away from her meal.

Once the female finds a hiding place, she settles in to eat. She plucks out the deer's hair to reach the hide. Then she chews her way into the body cavity and eats the liver, lungs, and kidneys. That way, if she is forced to give up her prey, she has already had the most nutritious parts. She continues eating, using her sharp teeth like scissors to snip off chunks of meat. When there is plenty of food, mountain lions are likely to gulp down from 20 to 30 pounds (9 to 13 kilograms) of meat during a meal.

After she's eaten her fill, meat is still left on the deer carcass. She scrapes leaf litter over it to cover it. Caching, or storing, the meat this way will help keep it cool and slow spoiling. It will also hide the kill from flying scavengers—animals that eat dead animals—such as crows and vultures. Wolves and grizzly bears often track these bird scavengers to find food to steal. If all goes well, the female mountain lion will be able to feed on her kill for at least another day.

Ready to rest, the big cat returns to her den, a sheltered ledge on a rocky hillside several miles away. On her own, she would stay near the kill to finish eating it, but two weeks earlier, she gave birth to two kittens—a male and a female. She returns to tend to them. When she reaches the den, she licks one kitten and then the other. They mew and look at her with their newly opened, kitten-colored, sky blue eyes.

The kittens scramble over each other, rushing to be first to latch onto one of their mother's nipples. Then they nurse. A female mountain lion's milk is like super-rich cream. This food gives the kittens the energy they need to grow quickly. By the time they're two months old, they'll weigh about 7 pounds (3 kg)—much more than their 1 pound (0.5 kg) birth weight. As soon as they're full, the kittens fall asleep.

Just a few days later, the mountain lion's instincts tell her it's time to move her family. Although most female mountain lions don't move their kittens until they're about eight weeks old, she has sensed a male mountain lion nearby. Male mountain lions are one of the biggest threats to the kittens. To them, the kittens are helpless prey. So she carries them—one at a time—in her mouth. The big cat's powerful jaws can bite to kill, but now she grips so gently her teeth don't even graze the kitten's skin.

Mountain lions spend most of their time asleep—as much as sixteen hours a day. So after the family is in its new home, the female naps again. The kittens wrestle and climb on their mother. Awakened, she hisses loudly at them.

The female mountain lion must kill prey to eat at least once a week. She needs about 10 pounds (4.5 km) of meat a day to get enough food energy to be active. She needs to eat even more while she is nursing her kittens. Whether prey is big or small, like this mule deer fawn, she first stalks it to get close. Then she pounces. She uses less energy when she waits to pounce on her prey, rather than running it down.

When the prey is big, like this adult bighorn sheep, it's worth the extra energy to chase it down. Killing bigger prey means she'll have a good supply of food. She can cache what's left after the first meal. Then she will be able to eat from her kill for two or three more days.

Not every hunt is successful, so mountain lions don't pass up hunting opportunities. When this raccoon ran up a tree, the female mountain lion climbed after it. But before she could knock it out of the tree with a paw swipe, the raccoon climbed even higher. It stays safe, perched on branches too small to support the big cat. The female mountain lion gives up and looks for easier hunting.

Mountain lions are one of the few predators that will even hunt porcupines. After the female knocked this porcupine out of a tree, she leaped down and flipped it onto its back. Only the porcupine's belly is free of quills. That's where the big cat bites to make her kill. Then she plucks the fur off the porcupine's belly with her teeth and tears into her meal. She leaves the hide and its quills behind when she's done eating.

While their mother
is away hunting, the
kittens mostly sleep.
When they are awake,
they explore and practice
climbing.

They also play with sticks or stalk each other and fight, practicing their hunting skills. Such rough play also helps them grow stronger. As adults, they'll fight to defend their kills. They may even fight for a home range.

Each mountain lion claims a home range, an area of land in which it lives and hunts. By having a home range, the mountain lion learns where to expect to find prey, such as deer, elk, or even ducks, in different seasons. It also learns the best routes to follow when chasing fast-running prey. Females find good den sites, where they will have their kittens.

The female lion moves her kitten once again. This time though, they are big enough to walk along with their mother to their new den site. They also begin to explore and learn about the home range that is their whole world.

Female mountain lions may have a home range as small as 50 square miles (130 sq. km). Males will have a home range as large as 150 square miles (390 sq. km). A male's range overlaps the home ranges of several females—possible mates.

At about eight weeks old, the kittens begin eating a little of the prey their mother kills. When she goes hunting, she leaves the kittens in thick vegetation or among rocks where they can hide. The kittens begin to nurse less often as their diet includes more meat. As the female mountain lion weans her youngsters, she has to hunt more often. The kittens need to eat more meat as they continue to grow. They also learn to develop a taste for the prey they'll soon hunt for themselves.

One day in September, it snows. Day after day, more snow falls, and most water freezes. During this time, the kittens' world changes, and so does the way they are living.

When they are about three months old, the kittens are weaned, meaning they no longer nurse. The female mountain lion often takes the kittens with her when she hunts. They wait nearby when she closes in to make a kill. Then they join her and share in the meal.

Throughout the winter, the mountain lion family moves regularly. The deer, elk, bighorn sheep, and other prey the female hunts are grazers. They have to travel to where the snow layer is thin, so they can feed on the grasses underneath it and browse on shrubs. The female mountain lion and her kittens follow. The youngsters are in training, learning where their mother hunts and how she stalks and ambushes prey. She still makes the kill alone, though.

Sometimes winter gives the female mountain lion an advantage. This old bighorn sheep had grown too weak to keep up with its herd. It no longer had the protection of being part of a group alert to approaching predators. It also couldn't run fast enough to escape. The female mountain lion easily chased down the old bighorn. She drags it to a secluded spot where she'll share it with her youngsters.

Winter may make hunting easier because prey animals will gather in places where they can find food. But having prey in one area also means there will likely be more hunters there too. The female mountain lion stays alert. When a coyote slips up and tries to steal meat from her kill, she chases the intruder away.

This hungry badger is not so easily scared off. The female mountain lion lays back her ears and stands her ground, snarling and spitting. Larger predators, such as a grizzly bear or a pack of wolves, could force her to give up her hard-earned meal, but not an animal as small as a badger. The badger finally gives up and waddles away.

By the time the kittens are five months old, they are losing their spots. They are beginning to look like young adults. But they'll still travel with their mother for at least the next six months. This way, they'll benefit from her protection and be sure of getting fed. While they continue to learn by watching their mother hunt, they'll also practice hunting on their own.

Nearly a year old, the young mountain lions are becoming experts at stalking and ambushing prey. Bounding after a hare, the young female snags her prey with claw-tipped paws. The young male is hunting successfully too. They both are ready to feed themselves.

In May, the adult female mountain lion goes off to hunt and never returns to her youngsters. Although the young mountain lions continue to hunt alone, for a while, they travel together. At first, they stay in their mother's home range. Then one day, the pair separates to hunt. The male keeps on traveling. He's beginning the search for his own home range.

He can tell what land is claimed because mountain lions leave scrapes to mark their boundaries. A scrape is a low mound of dirt and leaf litter a big cat pulls together. The mountain lion scent-marks this with its urine and dung. The young male's search for a home range continues day after day. Each day he rests and hunts. At first, he is most successful with smaller prey, like this beaver, which he can catch easily.

Many cats don't survive this first year on their own. But both the young male and female thrive. The female eventually leaves her mother's home range too, but she settles close by. The male needs to claim a much larger range, one that overlaps with that of several females. It will be another year or two, though, before he mates. The young female will be about two before she mates for the first time. In the meantime, both young mountain lions will perfect their hunting skills as they get to know their home ranges and its resources.

Shortly after she left her youngsters, the adult female mountain lion mated again. A little over three months later, she gives birth to a single kitten, a little male. Once again, she devotes herself fully to the job of raising another generation of hunters.

Looking Back

- Take another look at the cover to see the mountain lion's whiskers, sticking out of its cheeks on either side of its nose and above its eyes. These let the cat know how close things are around its face as it stalks prey through brush. When it pounces on its prey, the cat pulls its cheek whiskers forward to know when to sink in its teeth.

- Check out the mountain lion's tongue on page 12. It's covered with rough bumps that make it a good comb for grooming. It's also a good tool for helping to pull meat off bones and carrying water into the mountain lion's mouth.

- Take a close look at page 27 to see the kittens' blue eyes. Take another look at page 14 to see what color this big cat's eyes have become as an adult.

Glossary

AMBUSH: to make a surprise attack

CACHE: a hiding place. A mountain lion stores food in its cache.

DEN: the place where a mountain lion raises its young

HOME RANGE: the area within which an animal usually hunts. In the United States, mountain lions establish their home ranges within Florida plus the twelve westernmost states: California, Oregon, Washington, Idaho, Montana, Utah, Nevada, New Mexico, Arizona, Colorado, Texas, and Wyoming. Until the early 1900s, they could be found in a much larger area of the United States.

KITTEN: a young mountain lion

NURSE: to feed on milk from the mother's body

PREDATOR: an animal that hunts and kills other animals in order to live

PREY: an animal that a predator catches to eat

SCAVENGER: an animal that feeds on dead animals

STALK: to stealthily hunt for prey

WEAN: to encourage an animal to eat food other than milk

Further Information

Books

Barrett, Jalma. *Cougar.* Farmington Hills, MI: Blackbirch Press, 1998. In this book, investigate how the cougar or mountain lion survives in its environment.

Farentinos, Robert C. *Winter's Orphans: The Search for a Family of Mountain Lion Cubs.* Niwot, CO: Roberts Rinehart Publishers, 2001. The true story of a wildlife biologist's search for and rescue of orphaned mountain lion cubs after their mother's death.

George, Jean Craighead. *The Moon of the Mountain Lions.* New York: HarperCollins Children's Books, 1991. A Newbery award-winning author tells about a mountain lion's seasonal migration from the tree line of Mount Olympus to the Pacific coast.

Markle, Sandra. *Porcupines.* Minneapolis: Lerner Publications Company, 2006. Check out mountain lions from a prey animal's point of view.

Websites

Cougars
http://www.humboldt.net/~tracker/cougar.html
Listen to mountain lions and see their tracks.

Face to Face: Mountain Lions
http://www.nationalgeographic.com/ngkids/0401/
Discover how mountain lions and people learn to be neighbors.

San Diego Zoo: Mountain Lions
http://www.sandiegozoo.org/animalbytes/t-puma.html
Learn cool facts about these cats and how they live.

Index

For Dr. Gary Koehler, in appreciation for his research and efforts to protect these amazing big cats

The author would like to thank the following people for sharing their expertise and enthusiasm: Dr. Gary Koehler, Principal Investigator, Project C.A.T. (Cougars and Teaching), Washington Department of Fish & Wildlife; and Dr. Toni Ruth, Research Scientist, the Selway Institute and Wildlife Conservation Society. The author would also like to express a special thank-you to Skip Jeffery for his help and support during the creative process.

Photo Acknowledgments

The images in this book are used with the permission of: © Ronald Wittek/Photographer's Choice/Getty Images, p. 1; © Daniel J. Cox/NaturalExposures.com, p. 3; © W. Perry Conway/CORBIS, pp. 4, 7; © Mary Ann McDonald/CORBIS, p. 6; © Tom and Pat Leeson, pp. 9, 19; © D. Robert & Lori Franz/CORBIS, p. 10; © Kitchin & Hurst/leesonphoto, p. 11; © Rich Kirchner, p. 12; © Lukasseck/ARCO/naturepl.com, p. 13; © Tim Fitzharris/Minden Pictures, p. 14; © Erwin and Peggy Bauer, pp. 15, 23, 33; © Tom Brakefield/Photodisc/Getty Images, p. 16; © STOUFFER PRODUCTIONS/Animals Animals, p. 17; © C.C. LOCKWOOD/Animals Animals, p. 18; © Alan & Sandy Carey/zefa/CORBIS, p. 20; © Gavriel Jecan/Digital Vision/Getty Images, p. 21; © Jim and Jamie Dutcher/National Geographic/Getty Images, p. 22; © Norbert Rosing/National Geographic/Getty Images, p. 25; © kevinschafer.com, p. 26; © Joe McDonald, pp. 27, 29, 31; © Tom Brakefield/CORBIS, pp. 30, 35; © T. Kitchin and V. Hurst/NHPA/Photoshot, p. 32; © Frank Lukasseck/CORBIS, p. 34; © Terry W. Eggers/CORBIS, p. 37.
Cover: © Joe McDonald/CORBIS.

Lerner Publications Company
A division of Lerner Publishing Group, Inc.
241 First Avenue North
Minneapolis, MN 55401 U.S.A.

Website address: www.lernerbooks.com

Websites listed in Further Reading are current at the time of publication.

Library of Congress Cataloging-in-Publication Data

Markle, Sandra.
    Mountain lions / by Sandra Markle.
        p.   cm. — (Animal predators)
    Includes bibliographical references and index.
    ISBN-13: 978-1-58013-538-2 (lib. bdg. : alk. paper)
    1. Puma—Juvenile literature. I. Title.
QL737.C23M27244 2010
599.75'24—dc22   2008038123

Manufactured in the United States of America
1 2 3 4 5 6 – DP – 15 14 13 12 11 10